13 REASONS WHY NOT TO KILL YOURSELF

CONTACT LISA HANSON

Lisa is a powerful evangelist, author, worship leader, faith builder, wife, and mother. She flows in the gifts of the spirit & is used by God in the gifts of healing, prophecy, and demonstrating deliverance to captives. She preaches daily on her Facebook channels and in Revivals across the nation. You can see Lisa preach in person most Sundays at her church, Hope Center in Santa Fe, Tennesee. Lisa is available to minister at your event time permitting and God allowing. Send Inquiries VIA:

preachitlisa@gmail.com

www.PreachItLisa.com

https://www.facebook.com/13ReasonsWhyNotToKillYourself/
https://www.facebook.com/HopeCenterTrainingCenter/

- facebook.com/lisahansonministries
- twitter.com/preachitlisa
- instagram.com/preachitlisa
- tiktok.com/@preachitlisa

13 REASONS WHY NOT TO KILL YOURSELF

A NOTE FOR SUICIDE PREVENTION

LISA HANSON

Without limiting the rights under copyright(s) reserved below, no part of this publication may be reproduced, stored in or introduced into a retrieval system, or transmitted, in any form, or by any means (electronic, mechanical, photocopying, recording, or otherwise) without the prior permission of the publisher and the copyright owner.

The content of this book is provided "AS IS." The Publisher and the Author make no guarantees or warranties as to the accuracy, adequacy or completeness of or results to be obtained from using the content of this book, including any information that can be accessed through hyperlinks or otherwise, and expressly disclaim any warranty expressed or implied, including but not limited to implied warranties of merchantability or fitness for a particular purpose. This limitation of liability shall apply to any claim or cause whatsoever whether such claim or cause arises in contract, tort, or otherwise. In short, you, the reader, are responsible for your choices and the results they bring.

The scanning, uploading, and distributing of this book via the internet or via any other means without the permission of the publisher and copyright owner is illegal and punishable by law. Please purchase only authorized copies, and do not participate in or encourage piracy of copyrighted materials. Your support of the author's rights is appreciated.

Scripture quotations marked (NIV) are taken from the Holy Bible, New International Version®, NIV®. Copyright © 1973, 1978, 1984, 2011 by Biblica, Inc.™ Used by permission of Zondervan. All rights reserved worldwide. www.zondervan.comThe "NIV" and "New International Version" are trademarks registered in the United States Patent and Trademark Office by Biblica, Inc.™

Scripture quotations marked (ESV) are from The ESV® Bible (The Holy Bible, English Standard Version®), copyright © 2001 by Crossway, a publishing ministry of Good News Publishers. Used by permission. All rights reserved.

Copyright © 2019, 2021 by Hanson Ministries International. All rights reserved.

Book design by eBook Prep
www.ebookprep.com

May 2022
ISBN: 978-1-64457-288-7

Rise UP Publications
644 Shrewsbury Commons Ave
Ste 249
Shrewsbury PA 17361
United States of America
www.riseUPpublications.com
Phone: 866-846-5123

CONTENTS

An Important Message	13
Introduction	15
Reason #1 *No One Can Control Your Life*	19
Reason #2 *You Are Stronger Than The Words Of Others*	25
Reason #3 *Mistakes Are Just That...A MISTAKE*	29
Reason #4 *Words Do NOT Define You*	33
Reason #5 *You Are Not An Accident*	37
Reason #6 *Your Feelings Will Pass*	41
Reason #7 *No Matter Who Has Hurt You, It's Fixable*	45
Reason #8 *Not Every Voice You Hear Is Your Own*	51
Reason #9 *Look At Your Thumbprint You Have Purpose*	55
Reason #10 *If You've Been Deeply Hurt You Can Move On*	59
Reason #11 *Loneliness is Temporary*	63
Reason #12 *What About Them?*	67
Reason #13 *Suicide is...*	71
Say These Things	77
If You Need Help Now…	81
About the Author	82

In this book I share many personal and painful experiences. I've forgiven everyone involved.

LISA HANSON

To my husband, Chad, and my daughter, Matilda, who pray for me endlessly and without whom I could not minister to those who are hurting and broken.

You both are the most important people in my life; I'm so thankful for your prayers and support. May God bless you for everything you do.

...I have set before you life and death, blessings and curses. Now choose life, so that you and your children may live...

DEUTERONOMY 30:19 (NIV)

AN IMPORTANT MESSAGE

YOU have a person who cares about you, ME. Things are not as bad as you think. YOU can make it. This WILL pass.

I wrote this book for YOU, and I hope you will take a few minutes to read through it.

I've known people, some have even been my friends, who died of suicide. It makes me very angry because I know there is a "voice" that lies, but I want YOU to know the truth.

I use some references to the Bible in this book, but YOU do not need to be religious to get help from this book. Seriously it's OK if you are not.

So PLEASE read it. Please take time to look it over. YOU are worth it; YOUR LIFE IS worth it.

When you finish reading it, please write to me and tell me you've made it. I am praying for you, and I believe in you!

Lisa

INTRODUCTION

Why am I writing this book? This past year I've seen over and over many people take their own lives. After they are gone, I see their loved ones weeping.

There are many books written about the signs to look for and how to stop someone from ending their life, etc. There are very FEW books written DIRECTLY TO YOU, someone wanting to end their own life. This book is that book. This is a direct note to YOU.

My father was an abusive drunk who abused me throughout life. He'd say things like…

"You're a nobody."

"You'll never do anything."

"You'll go nowhere in life."

"You're stupid."

INTRODUCTION

He cussed at me and mentally abused me. He poured beer over my head when I was barely 5 years old, and much more.

He cussed me out one night as a teenage girl saying, "You're not my daughter!" When I found my "real" dad, I learned my biological dad wanted nothing to do with me, even though he had other daughters of his own.

I'm telling you this because I know what it's like to feel helpless, broken, abused, and unwanted. I've made it through; I've survived. That's how I KNOW there is hope for you.

Even if your situation is worse than mine was, I promise you there is hope. Please take a minute and read this note. I call it an anti-suicide note.

I'm not sharing tips or strategies. Please think of this book as your Anti-Suicide note. A note from me to you. Please, I plead with you to read this. I care for your life very much. Things will get better.

I am not a medical doctor. I am not a psychiatrist. This book is not intended to give medical advice. I am a wife, a mom, a minister who loves people, and I love YOU.

I believe God wanted me to write this book for you. To show you that you have a purpose. He has a plan for you. Even if you don't know HIM.

Right now, even if you don't have a religious bone in your body, it's OK. All I am asking for is just a few minutes or

INTRODUCTION

an hour or so (not sure how long this book may take) out of your day to read these simple truths.

After you read this, I'm asking you to make a choice. A choice to LIVE.

There are many books for other people. This book is for YOU.

May your heart be open, your mind healed, and your life long. I hope you will write to me and tell me: I chose LIFE. #IchoseLife

I believe in YOU. I'm praying for you.

If you're thinking about suicide, are worried about a friend or loved one, or want emotional support, see below for additional crisis services and hotlines.

National Suicide Prevention Lifeline
Call 1-800-273-8255
Available 24 hours every day

The Lifeline (@800273TALK) · Twitter
https://twitter.com/800273TALK

REASON #1

NO ONE CAN CONTROL YOUR LIFE

Sometimes people do things to us that are so terrible it seems impossible to recover. You might feel like life will never get better, and the hurt will never end.

But that is a lie!

When I was growing up, my dad said some pretty awful things to me. He used to say something like:

"You're going to grow up and be nothing."

"You can't do anything right."

"You are just here to pick up after your brothers."

"You are stupid!"

"You sit around like you're some queen, but you're not."

My dad had nothing good to say about me or to me.

When I was about 13, he cussed at me and told my mom to get me out of his house. He said I wasn't his daughter anyway.

Did it hurt? Yup. Did it suck? Yes, it did.

Did I cry? Yes, for hours, and many times.

But when I look back, as terrible as that moment was, if I had taken my life in any of those awful moments, I would not be writing this book for you. I wouldn't be here with my beautiful daughter.

I wouldn't be running through country fields or singing worship songs to Jesus. I wouldn't be loving my husband, or hugging a friend, or eating chocolate—we all need to eat more chocolate!

So this is what I want you—WAIT, I NEED YOU—to understand… If someone lies about you, verbally abuses you, takes or fakes a suggestive picture of you, the only power they have is the power you give them.

Does what they did hurt? Yes. Will you cry? Maybe. Can you recover from these things? YES, you can.

Another short story: When I was in high school, I made the mistake of riding with a guy on the way to spring break. I liked him, but he had a girlfriend. He made some advances that made me very uncomfortable. I stopped him, but we were alone, so no one knew the truth of what happened—or I should say what did NOT happen—except him and me. BUT that did not stop him from telling his girlfriend that I tried to "be" with him.

What happened? Well, she and all her friends gave me nasty looks for weeks at school. No one would speak to me; they all hated me. They would walk down the halls pretending I was invisible. It would have been easier if they just gave me hateful looks, but they walked past as if I was not there.

Did it hurt? Yes. Was I upset? Yes. Was it unfair? Yes.

But guess what? NONE of those people I went to school with ever went on to do half of what I've done. I've invented a product, traveled the world singing, written some books, lived on a beautiful farm, and have a great life. I'm not saying these things out of pride. I'm telling you that packed inside of you are gifts and a destiny more extraordinary than you can imagine.

You have a purpose. God has a plan. You are loved. And your enemies cannot cause your life to end. YOU are the only one with that power. Don't allow some fool to steal your future and rob you of your destiny.

BIBLE VERSES:

> For I know the plans I have for you,"
> declares the Lord, "plans to prosper you
> and not to harm you, plans to give you
> hope and a future.
>
> JEREMIAH 29:11 (NIV)

> Though I walk in the midst of trouble, you preserve my life. You stretch out your hand against the anger of my foes; with your right hand you save me.
>
> PSALM 138:7 (NIV)

SAY THESE THINGS:

- I refuse to let another person control me.
- There is an incredible plan for my life.
- I have a destiny.
- I have a purpose.
- I will laugh, I will smile, I will win.
- I will not allow the cruel actions of some person to rob me of my future.
- I am the only one in control of my life.
- I will live and not die.

REASON #2

YOU ARE STRONGER THAN THE WORDS OF OTHERS

I remember my dad saying hurtful things. Growing up, my friends would sometimes be mean or bully me. Sometimes they refused to play with me or called me names. Many times in elementary school, in junior high and high school, I dealt with days of anxiety and sometimes weeks of feeling rejected.

Does this sound like what you are going through?

Homework that seemed so easy for some, I'd sit for hours crying, trying to figure it out, while those who pretended to help me would tell me I just wasn't that smart. I thought I wasn't that smart, but that was a lie.

Maybe you've heard the same lies about yourself.

At the time, those moments were painful. I'm guessing much like the pain you feel now.

I'm telling you that **it will pass no matter how bad you feel right now.** The person turning people against you is really **nothing in your life.** Five years from now, you probably won't remember their name. I think it was a famous singer, she had a great saying, "If it won't matter 5 years from now it really doesn't matter" And honestly most things don't matter at all in 5 years.

I know this seems crazy. But as I'm writing this, I've never gone to even one of my high school reunions. Why? Because I didn't care about them. I don't have any good memories. In fact, I don't really have any memories of them.

Every day comes and goes and I never once think of a bad moment in high school or middle school where a person hurt me. I don't give the people I went to school with a second thought. Why? Because I've forgotten them, and I've forgiven them.

And you will too. No matter what is said. No matter what you feel, it will pass.

> Therefore, if anyone is in Christ, he is a
> new creation. The old has passed away;
> behold, the new has come.
>
> 2 CORINTHIANS 5:17 (ESV)

You may not realize this right now, but there is a way you can be free. You can let go of the nagging voice telling you that you are no good. I really wish I'd had a person like myself telling me I'd be OK back when I felt like crap. But now I get to tell you…

You will be OK!

I PROMISE. How do I know? Because I did. So If I can forget the pain in my past I promise you can too. You can let go, move on and forget the pain others are causing you.

Besides, if those causing you pain don't change their ways, they are the ones who will ultimately be hurt.

> A man who is kind benefits himself, but a
> cruel man hurts himself.
>
> PROVERBS 11:17 (ESV)

SAY THESE THINGS:

- I am free from anxiety.
- I am filled with peace.
- I declare that any feeling of hopelessness leaves my heart right now!
- I have a great destiny.
- God is for me.
- I am the only one in control of my own life.
- I will live and not die.

REASON #3
MISTAKES ARE JUST THAT...A MISTAKE

I'm not a fan of screwing up. I've done it many times, and it's not my favorite thing at all.

That being said, here is a great truth for you to grab:

You are going to screw up!

You will make a mistake or possibly many mistakes. Some will be big, others will be small. Some will be humiliating, while others are no big deal. But mistakes do not and will not define your future.

If God can forgive you, why can't you forgive yourself?

You can.

"Well you don't understand what they are saying about me."

"You didn't see the messages they are passing around or the pictures."

And to all this, I say to you, "So what?"

Unless you give that person permission to hurt you, these things cannot hurt you.

Yes, you made a mistake. I'm guessing it was embarrassing. But it's not the first or last time you'll ever make a mistake, and your life is a lot more valuable than one mistake.

Maybe your mistake is so big you are facing a major consequence. It's OK; there is always hope. You can't even imagine the good things that will happen in your future.

Do not give up!

> For as high as the heavens are above the
> earth, so great is his love for those who
> fear him;...
>
> PSALM 103:11 (NIV)

Every day that you wake up, you have a choice. You can keep going, or you can quit. You can allow your mistakes to define you, or we can say, "You know what? That was stupid. I shouldn't have done that. I'll do better next time."

Because guess what? **THERE CAN BE A NEXT TIME.** So don't get so upset with your mistake that you allow it to tell you what should happen in your life.

Think of just one "right thing" you have done. It could be as simple as I brush my teeth, comb my hair, smile sometimes, or I was kind to an animal or a friend or…well, you fill in the blank.

Now focus on that "right thing" and…

SAY THESE THINGS:

- It's not the bad things in my life that define me. It's how I come out of those moments.
- I will not be stopped. I will not give up.
- A mistake is just a mistake.
- I'll get up, I'll keep going, and I will not hurt myself.
- I am a good person, and I will keep trying.
- It doesn't matter what other people say.
- I'm in control of my future.
- I have hope.
- I forgive myself. I choose life!

REASON #4

WORDS DO NOT DEFINE YOU

When a person says something extremely hurtful, what do you do? What if what they say has some truth? What if it doesn't? Either way, I want you to remember this statement…

Any words a person speaks OUTSIDE of your soul and spirit do NOT define who you are INSIDE.

Rumors hurt. Words hurt. BUT when these things happen, we have a choice. You see, it's always YOUR choice to receive hurt and pain, not theirs.

You could buckle under the pressure, cry, do something irrational or stupid, or you can take a deep breath and say, **"WAIT a minute, these words do not define who I am on the inside. I will not allow cruel words spoken by another person to rob me of my amazing future.** I may not know what my future holds, but I know it's better than what is happening today. I will not forfeit my destiny over words or lies spoken over me today. I will **CHOOSE LIFE.**

> …for God gave us a spirit not of fear but of power and love and self-control.
>
> 2 TIMOTHY 1:7 (ESV)

> I can do all things through him who strengthens me.
>
> PHILIPPIANS 4:13 (ESV)

I want to tell you the story of a man. He was a murderer, and he did some pretty awful things. But when his heart was changed, so was he. People still talked about him because they remembered who he **used to be.** But he said, "I am not going to think about that. I'm going to focus on good things in front of me." That man wrote some of the most powerful things in history. If he can do that, what can you do?

Now, what if he had fallen to the ground crying, "They are talking about me!" What if he had given up? Well, then, the world would never have received all the great gifts he brought.

So I promise you, if you don't give up, if you don't quit, if you stand up and say, **"I will not allow these words to define who I am."**

I promise your future will be bright.

SAY THESE THINGS:

- I will not allow the cruelty of others to rob me of my future.
- Words spoken on the outside can not stop my destiny on the inside
- They are broken for speaking like that, I am not, I am strong.
- I am not afraid. I have a great future, and I'm not giving it up, no matter what others say.
- I have strength in my heart, peace in my mind and laughter in my heart.
- I choose life.

REASON #5

YOU ARE NOT AN ACCIDENT

In this short time you and I are hanging out, I don't want you to have any preconceived ideas. If you're not into faith, it's OK; everything I share will still help you and could save your incredibly amazing life.

Maybe you are thinking, "How would you even know? Who are you anyway?"

So let's figure that out first.

I grew up in a home with a raging drunk dad. He screamed at me almost every day of my life. He told me I was stupid, lazy, and would never be anything, go anywhere, or do anything in life. Fun, right? LOL No.

One cold Michigan night, drunk out of his mind, he told my mother, "Get that BLEEP out of my house. She's not my daughter anyway."

That was the day and the way I found out I had another dad—my real dad. Cool, right? Wrong!

It turned out that my REAL dad, well, he didn't want me either—not even a little bit.

I've also been through many broken relationships. I've done some pretty awful things, many things I regret. But I came through to the other side, and so can you.

I'm telling you this so you know that I too have dealt with a lot of rejection, anger, and abuse. Maybe you have, or maybe you haven't, but either way, we all have thoughts that land in our brains. Thoughts that are not good. Thoughts that try to make us feel like garbage. The key to life is not what happens TO us, but what we do with these thoughts and how we thrive THROUGH them.

Now you know that I didn't have a perfect childhood and I dealt with some pretty sucky thoughts. Now, lets get back to where I said YOU ARE NOT AN ACCIDENT.

> "Before I formed you in the womb I knew you, and before you were born I consecrated you; I appointed you a prophet to the nations."
>
> JEREMIAH 1:5 (ESV)

It doesn't matter if you were told that you were a mistake or unplanned or were conceived in the back seat of a car. It doesn't matter if you were raised by loving parents, divorced parents, or two people who barely knew each other. God planned you. Before the beginning of time, He knew you. This means you have a SPECIFIC DESTINY that you are created to fill. And without you, the world will not be as great as it could have been.

YOU MATTER IN A BIG WAY.

Whether you believe in HIM or not doesn't change the fact that HE BELIEVES IN YOU. Whether your mom and dad knew about His plan for you or not doesn't matter because GOD DID NOT NEED THEIR PERMISSION TO MAKE A PLAN FOR YOU.

SAY THESE THINGS:

- I'm not an accident.
- I have a purpose.
- I have an amazing destiny.
- I'm going to choose life to find out what that destiny is.

REASON #6
YOUR FEELINGS WILL PASS

Have you ever watched the water? If not go and look at ocean waves. If you are not next to an ocean, you can just YouTube it.

Those waves come and they go. That is exactly how our emotions are. Honestly, sometimes they cannot be trusted. Emotions are just what they are called, MOTION. Motions move and change. Are you upset? Feeling rejected? Lonely? Feeling left out or used? Feeling unloved or unwanted or misunderstood? Every one of these emotions WILL pass. It's not that these feelings aren't real, it's that these real feelings will PASS.

So if your emotions change like the ocean waves, why make a decision in the middle of a bad emotion? Wouldn't it be really lousy to do something harmful in the middle of feeling sorry for yourself, especially if tomorrow something great could be waiting for you, right?

Here are some secrets. This voice in your head that says stupid things to you like, "You're alone, and no one cares," has whispered the same thing to a lot of people. BUT don't let that voice win! Tell that voice to SHUT UP!

Whether it's people being mean to you or making fun of how you look or whatever, THIS WILL PASS. When I was in high school, not many people liked me. I wasn't the girl with the best clothes or the best hair or the best anything. I was average. Other kids could be really mean. A lot of the time I felt pretty lousy about myself. BUT if I had done anything to harm myself, then I couldn't talk to you now. It's strange how someone thought you are that valuable; and you are.

And a funny thing, many of the kids in my school never went on to do half of the things that I have. Of course, some had success but understand what I'm saying. If you let the voices stop you now, you're going to miss all the amazing and cool things you can do in life.

Maybe you don't know this, but there is already a GREAT PLAN FOR YOUR FUTURE. How do I know this

Check this out:

> "For I know the plans I have for you,"
>   declares the Lord, "plans to prosper you
>   and not to harm you, plans to give you
>   hope and a future."
>
>   JEREMIAH 29:11 (NIV)

13 REASONS WHY NOT TO KILL YOURSELF

Knowing there is already a plan set in motion is pretty awesome! You are not alone. You are not the only person to feel junky from time to time or have people be mean to you. As a matter of fact, people being mean to other people has been going on forever. And it's really getting old, don't you think? I mean, what gives anyone the right to determine what YOU do with YOUR life?

Say These Things To Your Feelings:

- Shut up. You don't have a right to tell me what to do.
- These lonely feelings will pass.
- This pain will leave
- I have a purpose.
- I am loved.
- I have a destiny.
- You can't harm me.
- I refuse to harm myself.
- So, SHUT UP!

There, doesn't that feel better? You have a purpose, and it's pretty amazing!

REASON #7

NO MATTER WHO HAS HURT YOU, IT'S FIXABLE

Maybe someone has done something so awful that you think you will never recover. I want to offer you hope; you can recover. How do I know this? There was a great woman whose dad sexually molested her from childhood until she became a teenager. As horrifying as this was, she wrote many, many books, and she speaks worldwide. She encourages other women and men and has a great family and a beautiful life. She's alive to tell the story.

When we allow the hurt that another person has caused us to determine if we live or die, guess what? They win. But they're not worth it. There is no hurt too deep, no pain too big, nothing has happened to you that God can't help you overcome—that YOU cannot overcome.

> The LORD is close to the brokenhearted
> and saves those who are crushed in
> spirit.
>
> PSALM 34:18 (NIV)

> "Be strong and courageous. Do not be
> afraid or terrified because of them, for
> the Lord your God goes with you; he
> will never leave you nor forsake you"
>
> DEUTERONOMY 31:6 (NIV)

> "For I know the plans I have for you,"
> declares the Lord, "plans to prosper you
> and not to harm you, plans to give you
> hope and a future."
>
> JEREMIAH 29:11 (NIV)

So, you're faced with a choice: You can let pain and hurt define you or you can look up and say, "NO! What happened to me will not ruin the rest of my life! That was NOT my fault,"—even IF it may have been your fault, God can still erase your pain.

There was a man in the Bible his name was Paul. But he started out with a different name; he was called Saul. He was mean, and he often told people they were wrong; then, he'd find and kill them. This man thought he was doing right, but he was not. One day Jesus had a talk with him and changed his life forever. Jesus changed his name from Saul to Paul. This ex-murderer wrote 2/3 of the New Testament in The Bible.

If Paul had always looked back at how bad he'd been, he could never have written a passage like this:

> Love is patient, love is kind. It does not envy, it does not boast, it is not proud. It does not dishonor others, it is not self-seeking, it is not easily angered, it keeps no record of wrongs. Love does not delight in evil but rejoices with the truth. It always protects, always trusts, always hopes, always perseveres. Love never fails. But where there are prophecies, they will cease; where there are tongues, they will be stilled; where there is knowledge, it will pass away.
>
> 1 CORINTHIANS 13:4-8 (NIV)

He is telling you that LOVE will never fail. God LOVES you; He is FOR you, not against you. So LOVE yourself and resolve that your past will not determine your future. Maybe you don't believe in God, but HE BELIEVES In YOU. Choose LIFE!

SAY THESE THINGS:

- No matter what mistakes I've made, I know God loves me.
- Pain caused by others will not define my future.
- I am courageous.
- I am strong.
- I will speak up and share my life so I can help others.
- I never give up.
- I never quit.

REASON #8

NOT EVERY VOICE YOU HEAR IS YOUR OWN

Sometimes we hear thoughts in our heads…"You are ugly, you are stupid, it would be easier if it was over." Those are not good voices. The good news is that those thoughts are not really your thoughts. You need to know that not every voice in your head is your own.

You might be thinking, "Lisa, that's crazy; how can you say that? I hear it in my head; of course, it's mine." No, it is not. Let me show you some examples because sometimes it's a bad spirit or bad memory in your head; it is not your own thought.

> For we do not wrestle against flesh and blood, but against the rulers, against the authorities, against the cosmic powers over this present darkness, against the spiritual forces of evil in the heavenly places.
>
> EPHESIANS 6:12 (ESV)

This passage says you are not in a fight with people. Other people are not the problem; you're not the problem—sometimes there are influences from other places. When you realize this fact, you will understand that these voices are not from you or FOR you. This isn't some strange woo-woo thing—it's for real.

If you have ideas or thoughts of harming yourself or anyone else, you must resist such things. Thoughts like this come from spiritual forces meaning to destroy you.

SAY THESE THINGS:

- I will not listen to thoughts of harm.
- I am amazing! I am smart! I am strong!
- I will live a long life! I AM worthy.
- I have a purpose.
- I choose LIFE.

What happens when you speak these things out loud? I know it may seem weird that outside forces influence you. When you speak against them, bad feelings leave because they must.

I promise that your life has purpose and meaning. If you were gone, even though you don't believe it right now, people would really miss you.

And if you are still saying, "No, there would not be," well, let me tell you, if I read about you online or in the news and you were not here, I would be very sad. Because I know God loves you, and there are so many wonderful things you can do with your life.

Never give up! Find something today that makes you smile. Go outside, look at a pretty animal, pet a dog, or look up to Heaven and smile. But do not give up. I know you can make it. At the beginning of this chapter is a picture of my dog Elsa, who we wouldn't have if I wasn't here. Somewhere, there's a dog who needs you too. Or a cat or a fish, but some animal somewhere needs you.

REASON #9

LOOK AT YOUR THUMBPRINT YOU HAVE PURPOSE

This may sound weird but look at your thumb. Go ahead, I'll wait…just do it.

No two thumbprints in the whole wide world are the same. Your thumbprint was created inside the womb. And it's as if God stamped you saying, **"I created you."**

You are special, You are unique. There is NO other person like you on the planet.

If you decided not to be around any longer, you would leave a massive void on earth that only you could fill. Why?

There is not a single human being like you, and no one can take your place. That means there is a purpose, and you are the only one who can fulfill it. If you've ever struggled with feeling useless, if you've ever felt purposeless, remember this: Just because you have not yet discovered your purpose doesn't mean you don't have one.

I promise that you have a purpose. You are literally one of a kind. You have a particular purpose. So look at your thumb again and…

SAY THESE THINGS:

- This thumbprint means I am one of a kind.
- I am special.
- I am unique.
- There is no one else like me in the whole wide world.
- It doesn't matter if my qualities are cool or quirky. They belong to ME. God knew it when He made me, even if I don't know HIM yet.
- So I tell myself, SELF, you are OK.
- I have a great future.
- I will not be sad. I will not give up. I will never let go.
- I will LIVE on. I will MOVE on. I will GET on.
- I am really special.
- Whenever I doubt myself, I will look at my thumb and remember how unique and special I truly am.

REASON #10

IF YOU'VE BEEN DEEPLY HURT YOU CAN MOVE ON

Sometimes we think we are the only person in the world in emotional pain; this is that lying voice speaking. But I can assure you that many people have been hurt. You are built to be tougher than you think. You can bounce back in ways you can't even imagine. No matter what pain you are feeling, there is a special DNA already created inside you that helps you overcome. If I took you to the middle of the ocean and threw you overboard, even if you are contemplating hurting yourself, instinctively, you would try to swim. You would not just effortlessly sink to the bottom. Why is that? Because you were predesigned with a will to **SURVIVE**.

My biological dad wants nothing to do with me. It hurts, but should I ruin my own life because he is stupid? Of course not. And no matter what has happened to you, don't allow your future to be ruined. Forgive people. Forgive yourself and CHOOSE LIFE.

I've experienced pain in different ways, maybe like you. Sometimes people said they loved me. I've had boyfriends and bad situations where they clearly did not love me; maybe a relationship hurt you too. I was deeply hurt and felt incredibly rejected, but I would not have the awesome, loving husband I have now if I had given up. If I'd given up, I wouldn't have the coolest daughter in the world. You CAN overcome. I don't care if no other person on earth is telling you this. I AM TELLING YOU THAT YOU MUST LIVE. DON'T GIVE UP. CHOOSE LIFE.

I'm not making light of your pain or telling you to stay with something painful like a bad relationship. I am not suggesting you hang out with a person who was cruel to you. It simply means you are the decision-maker.

When something awful happens, you have two roads to choose from:

1. Anger, bitterness, depression, sadness. (This road stinks, by the way)
2. Forgiveness, moving on, thriving, helping others. (CHOOSE this one)

There really are no other options. If you choose option 1, you give that person more power than they deserve. No matter how awful it was, never let the actions of others affect you for the rest of your life.

FORGIVE AND LIVE.

Even if YOU made a wrong decision and it IS your fault, FORGIVE YOURSELF. I promise you will feel much better.

Never give up. Never quit. You've got this!

SAY THESE THINGS:

- I refuse to give another person any power over my mind or my heart.
- The pain caused by others will NOT control me. Why in the world would I allow my life to be changed because of some terrible person?
- I have power over my life. I will thrive, I will live on, I will rise, I will overcome.

REASON #11

LONELINESS IS TEMPORARY

We live in a very connected world. You can check out Snapchat or Facebook, or Instagram, and chances are you will see a person you know. But social media is not a cure for loneliness; in fact, it can make people feel more alone. Maybe you think no one cares; to that, I say, "HERE I AM." Please, my new friend, let me tell you something: Many, many people care about YOU.

I have a question for you. Are you willing to let a **temporary** feeling like loneliness, hurt, abuse, or rejection drive you to a **permanent** decision? Please don't.

I've struggled to write this book. Not because I don't think you will read it or that it will help you, but because I also feel lonely at times. I'm in a very secluded season of life. My husband and child leave our house every day, and I am alone with my thoughts. Maybe it's the same for you.

Sometimes those thoughts tell you that you don't have a lot of friends or no one cares. But I don't believe that's true.

Loneliness is a real feeling. But you and I don't have to allow this feeling to make us think, "What am I here for? I guess I'll just leave."

The best thing you and I can do when we feel lonely is to get out of our own heads. We think about ourselves way too much. We need to GO somewhere. Find a place where people are hurting and smile at them. Go to a shelter and help an abandoned dog or cat. Watch something that makes us laugh. Go to the grocery store and help an elderly person. Just GO; it doesn't matter where, as long as you are not just sitting alone thinking. Get out of your own head.

Remind yourself that there are people who are waiting for you just to smile at them. They may feel just as lonely as you do.

I'm not saying this is an easy thing to do. When you are feeling lonely or are hurting, you probably just want to be alone…but that makes you more lonely—**trust me, I know.**

Just take one step today and do something for another person. Then tell me if you still feel lonely. Maybe comment on their post that they look great. Or you hope they have a great day. Or pet some cats that don't have a good home, or volunteer at the animal shelter. Trust me, those animals need your love.

Don't allow a temporary feeling of loneliness to make you do something permanent.

Know that you are very loved—I love you, and I know you can make it.

> When he calls to me, I will answer him; I will be with him in trouble; I will rescue him and honor him.
>
> PSALM 91: 15 (ESV)

SAY THESE THINGS:

- Loneliness is only temporary.
- People love me and care about me.
- I promise to smile at another person today who looks sad like me.
- I won't sit here and feel sorry for myself. I will go for a walk. I will go to the park. I will laugh.
- I am worthy of love. I promise to love myself.
- I will not allow a temporary feeling to make me do something permanent.
- I will CHOOSE LIFE TODAY.

REASON #12

WHAT ABOUT THEM?

What about "them"?

You may be thinking, what is this girl talking about. Who are "them"?

"Them" are all the people who will weep if you leave. "Them" are the people who will flood your social media with things like…

"I can't believe you are gone."

"I miss you so much."

"Why didn't you talk to me?"

"Them" is every single person who will be crushed and heartbroken for a very long time if you are no longer on this earth.

What about your mom?

Your dad?

Your Aunty?

Your kids?

Your wife or husband?

Maybe you don't have these people in your life but what about a friend? If you think about it, we all have that ONE person we know will be hurt if we were gone.

Listen to me carefully... If you go ahead and do this awful thing you are thinking about doing, they will find you, and they will mourn you. It will hurt them very, very deeply.

Maybe other people are afraid to tell you how much pain your suicide could cause. Maybe they fear telling you how hurt people will be if you decide to kill yourself. I guess they don't say things like this to you, perhaps thinking you may go deeper into depression. I'm not afraid. It's important you THINK about this and realize what your choices may do to another person.

I know that IF you did think about "them", you would realize what a terrible thing it would be for them to wake up and find you gone. There is so much you have yet to learn. So much you can do and see. But think about the impact on the lives of others if you make this choice.

Maybe you are thinking, "Lisa, seriously? Do I really need to know that?" YES. Yes, you do. Because your decision doesn't only affect you. It will cause a ripple effect that will mess up many lives.

Use your life to make a difference. Use your life to bless people. Use your life to love and laugh and explore everything this world offers. But do not allow a lying voice in your head to cause you to bring pain to others.

There are so many who think about you. Just because you don't realize it doesn't mean that they don't.

SAY THESE THINGS:

- I will not bring pain to anyone I love.
- I will not be a statistic.
- I'm going to come up out of this slump.
- I will use my life to make people laugh.
- I will use my life to bring joy.
- I refuse to allow a decision I make to hurt anyone else.
- I CHOOSE LIFE.

Did you say these things? Good! Then let's keep walking together.

REASON #13

SUICIDE IS...

Suicide is NOT the answer.

Suicide only causes GREATER problems for everyone else in life that you were ever around. It will not SOLVE anything. NO ONE is better off without you.

NO ONE will have more peace if you aren't here. YOU will not have peace if you aren't here; don't ever think you will!

And something I wish I didn't have to say...

Suicide Is Totally And Completely Selfish

This is possibly the most controversial chapter in this book. And to be honest, it's tough for me to write it.

IF you really thought about someone else instead of YOURSELF and everything you are going through, you would not—could not—take your own life.

I've seen countless fathers in the media, with gorgeous wives and children, take their lives. What do you think their young sons or daughters will deal with while they "relieved" their emotional discomfort?

What about your wife? Your husband? Your mom? Your brother or sister? Your friends? Just think of ONE person who will really be devastated. Do you want to put them through that?

You may be hurting right now. Maybe you think it's unbearable. I promise you it's NOT.

How do I know? Because millions before you went through the exact same pain and are still here. There is a lie that you are the only one feeling like you do but that's not true. Others were abused the same, yelled at the same, rejected the same, isolated the same, lost the same things, and guess what? They are living, loving, and laughing.

It's a lie that you are the only one to feel the way you feel.

I can't stop you from killing yourself. BUT IF YOU DO, IT WON'T FIX ANYTHING, and you will miss out on so many amazing things in this world.

I promise you are not alleviating anyone's pain by doing it. NOT your own and definitely not anyone else's around you. You will cause a HUGE amount of pain for others.

Do you really want that? I'm hoping the answer is NO.

So I want you to really picture the thing you were thinking about. Now think about the poor person who has to find you in that state. Do you really want them to see that? NO you don't.

Suicide is a lying voice. And you **MUST tell it to SHUT UP AND LEAVE**. There is no way you can do this thing because it's stupid, hurtful, deeply wounding to others, and YOU will MISS out on so many amazing things.

This is the final thing I want to leave you with. Suicide may not be all in your head. It may be something from the outside trying to influence you.

Can you try something for me?

I said you don't need a religion, and you don't. But please hear me out... Life without Jesus is very lonely. He came to this earth, and everywhere He traveled, He loved people who were broken and hurting, and He always helped people.

This simple truth is life-changing and life-saving. Jesus helped parents with broken hearts, people with broken bodies, others with broken minds, and HE CAN help you too. If you let HIM.

> For God so loved the world that he gave his one and only Son, that whoever believes in him shall not perish but have eternal life.
>
> JOHN 3:16 (NIV)

Jesus came to take away whatever pain or anxiety you feel, but you need to ASK Him to take it away. Even if you don't do this right now, start by reading the confessions throughout this book. I know they will help you. When you are ready to ASK Jesus for help, it's really simple. Just speak this:

> Jesus, Forgive me for my mistakes.
> Please help me, come into my heart and change my mind.
> Be the Lord of my life…HELP ME, JESUS.
> AMEN

If you say that simple statement, you will start feeling much better.

SAY THESE THINGS:

- You spirit of suicide, I do NOT want you. I do NOT need your voice speaking to me. I command you to leave me right now IN JESUS NAME. I command you to stop harassing my mind and my heart. LEAVE ME NOW and never speak to my mind again!
- I didn't think about other people; I didn't realize they would be wounded or so sad. I thought I was helping, but now I see I'd only hurt more people
- I'm making a different choice…a better choice.
- I'm NOT going to take my own life

- I'm going to message LISA right now and tell her: Today is a new day for me
- I choose life!

MESSAGE ME RIGHT NOW ...

http://www.Facebook.com/LisaHansonMinistries

Tell me that you decided to live.

Let me know that YOU Chose Life on Instagram or Twitter or Facebook. Use #IChoseLife @PreachItLisa

Tell me that you shut down those lying voices. I'm waiting for you; let me know.

SAY THESE THINGS

I've put all the things in the book in this one place. Speak them over yourself. Never lose hope. Don't give up. As you speak these I believe you will begin to feel a change.

- I refuse to let another person control me.
- There is a wonderful plan for my life.
- I have a destiny.
- I have a purpose.
- I will laugh, I will smile, I will win.
- I will not allow the cruel actions of another person to rob my future from me.
- I am the only one in control of my own life; I will live and not die.
- I am free from anxiety.
- I am filled with peace.
- Feelings of hopelessness must leave my heart right now!
- I have a great destiny.

- God is for me.
- The bad things in my life do not define me; it's how I come out of those moments.
- I will not give up.
- A mistake is just a mistake; I'll get up, I'll keep going, and I will not hurt myself.
- I am a good person, and I will keep trying.
- It doesn't matter what other people say.
- I'm in control of my future.
- I have hope.
- I forgive myself; I choose life.
- Words spoken on the outside can not stop my destiny on the inside.
- I am strong.
- I am not afraid. I have a great future. I'm not giving it up, no matter what others say.
- I have strength in my heart, peace in my mind, and laughter in my heart. Today is different.
- I'm not an accident; I'm on purpose.
- I have an amazing destiny.
- I will choose life to find out what that destiny is.
- Feelings of loneliness will pass.
- This pain will leave
- I am loved
- Others can't harm me, and I refuse to harm myself.
- No matter what mistakes I've made, God loves me.
- I am courageous.
- I am strong.

- I will speak up and share my life so I can help others.
- I never give up.
- I never quit.
- I am amazing! I am smart! I am strong!
- I will live a long life! I am worthy.
- This thumbprint means I am one of a kind.
- I am special.
- I am unique.
- There is no one else like me in the whole wide world.
- It doesn't matter if my qualities are cool or quirky.
- I have a great future.
- Live on. Move on. Get on.
- I am really special.
- Whenever I doubt myself, I will look at my thumb and remember how unique and special I truly am.
- I will not bring pain to anyone I love.
- I will not be a statistic.
- I'm going to come up out of this slump.
- I will use my life to make people laugh.
- I will use my life to bring joy.
- I refuse to allow a decision I make to hurt anyone else.
- I choose life.
- I'm making a different choice, a better choice.
- I'm not going to take my own life.
- I choose life!

I will be thinking about you and believing that you make a choice to live. Your future is bright. You are intelligent, bright and beautiful. You will not be alone. I am with you. Jesus is with you. NEVER forget.

Now, go do something amazing!

I want to watch you LIVE

Lisa

IF YOU NEED HELP NOW...

If you're thinking about suicide, are worried about a friend or loved one, or would like emotional support, see below for additional crisis services and hotlines.

National Suicide Prevention Lifeline
Call 1-800-273-8255
Available 24 hours every day
The Lifeline (@800273TALK) · Twitter
https://twitter.com/800273TALK

ABOUT THE AUTHOR

Lisa is a powerful evangelist, author, worship leader, faith builder, wife, and mother. She flows in the gifts of the spirit and is used by God through the gifts of healing, prophecy, and demonstrating deliverance to captives. She preaches daily on her Facebook channels and in Revivals across the nation. You can see Lisa preach in person most Sundays at her church, Hope Center in Santa Fe, Tennessee. By sharing her story of overcoming pain and rejection and hope and healing through the power of Christ, she has impacted people around the world.

Lisa is available to minister at your event time permitting and God allowing. Send Inquiries VIA:

preachitlisa@gmail.com

www.PreachItLisa.com

Follow Lisa On Social Media

https://www.facebook.com/13ReasonsWhyNotToKillYourself/

https://www.facebook.com/HopeCenterTrainingCenter/

- facebook.com/lisahansonministries
- twitter.com/preachitlisa
- instagram.com/preachitlisa
- tiktok.com/@preachitlisa

CPSIA information can be obtained
at www.ICGtesting.com
Printed in the USA
BVHW041414130522
636973BV00009B/294